NATIONAL GEOGRAPHIC | GLOBAL ISSUES

MIGRATION

Andrew J. Milson, Ph.D.
Content Consultant
University of Texas at Arlington

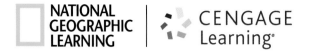

Acknowledgments

Grateful acknowledgment is given to the authors, artists, photographers, museums, publishers, and agents for permission to reprint copyrighted material. Every effort has been made to secure the appropriate permission. If any omissions have been made or if corrections are required, please contact the Publisher.

Instructional Consultant: Christopher Johnson, Evanston, Illinois

Teacher Reviewer: Andrea Wallenbeck, Exploris Middle School, Raleigh, North Carolina

Photographic Credits

Front Cover, Inside Front Cover, Title Page ©les polders/Alamy. **3** (bg) ©Santokh Kochar/Photodisc/Getty Images. **4** (bg) ©Danny Lehman/Corbis. **6** (bg) ©dbtravel/dbimages/Alamy. **8** (bg) Mapping Specialists. **10** (bg) ©Russell Gordon/DanitaDelimont.com/Newscom. **11** (tl) ©Jorge Rios Ponce/picture-alliance/dpa/Newscom. **13** (bg) ©Mark Henley/Impact/HIP/The Image Works. **14** (bg) ©Pablo Lopez Luz. **16** (bg) ©Keenpress/National Geographic Stock. **17** (bl) ©Anthony Cassidy/Photodisc/Getty Images. **18** (br) Mapping Specialists. **19** (bg) ©Guus Dubbelman/Reuters/Corbis. **20** (bg) ©Ton Koene/Picture Contact BV/Alamy. (tl) ©Ingolf Pompe/LOOK/Getty Images. **22** (bg) ©Mark Thiessen/National Geographic Stock. **25** (bg) ©David Evans. **27** (t) ©Blaine Harrington III/Corbis. **28** (tr) ©Radius Images/Getty Images. **30** (br) ©Anthony Bradshaw/Photodisc/Getty Images. (tr) ©Russell Gordon/DanitaDelimont.com/Newscom. **31** (bg) ©Santokh Kochar/Photodisc/Getty Images. (tr) ©Danny Lehman/Corbis. (bc) ©dbtravel/dbimages/Alamy. (br) ©Pablo Lopez Luz.

MetaMetrics® and the MetaMetrics logo and tagline are trademarks of MetaMetrics, Inc., and are registered in the United States and abroad. The trademarks and names of other companies and products mentioned herein are the property of their respective owners. Copyright © 2010 MetaMetrics, Inc. All rights reserved.

Visit National Geographic Learning online at www.NGSP.com.

Visit our corporate website at www.cengage.com.

Printed in the USA.

RR Donnelley, Menasha, WI

ISBN: 978-07362-97684

15 16 17 18 19 20 21

10 9 8 7 6 5 4 3

PEOPLE
ON THE
MOVE

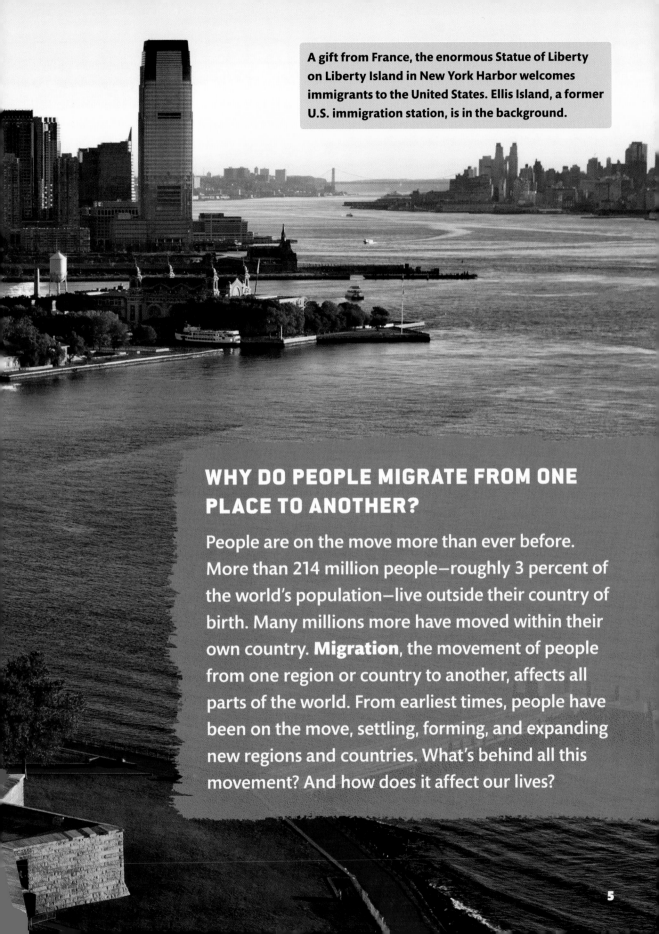

A gift from France, the enormous Statue of Liberty on Liberty Island in New York Harbor welcomes immigrants to the United States. Ellis Island, a former U.S. immigration station, is in the background.

WHY DO PEOPLE MIGRATE FROM ONE PLACE TO ANOTHER?

People are on the move more than ever before. More than 214 million people—roughly 3 percent of the world's population—live outside their country of birth. Many millions more have moved within their own country. **Migration**, the movement of people from one region or country to another, affects all parts of the world. From earliest times, people have been on the move, settling, forming, and expanding new regions and countries. What's behind all this movement? And how does it affect our lives?

STARTING OVER

Migrants are people who move from one region or country to another. **Immigrants** are people who move specifically to a new country. Some immigrants are unskilled workers. Others are scientists, doctors, engineers, teachers, and students.

Why would people uproot their lives and start over in a new place? Geographers often use the theory of push-pull factors to explain the reasons for migration. Push factors are conditions that *drive people away* from an area, such as a low standard of living or war. Pull factors are conditions that *attract people* to a new area, such as high-paying jobs and good schools.

Changi Airport in Singapore is a major center of activity for immigration in Southeast Asia. Centrally located, the airport handles regional traffic as well as overseas flights.

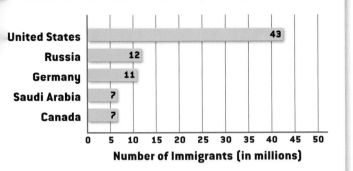

COUNTRIES WITH MOST IMMIGRANTS

United States: 43
Russia: 12
Germany: 11
Saudi Arabia: ?
Canada: ?

Number of Immigrants (in millions)

Source: Migration Policy Institute, 2010

GATEWAYS TO MIGRATION

The chief reason people move is to find jobs. So it makes sense that most international migration consists of people moving from poorer countries to wealthier countries. The majority of immigrants settle in cities and suburbs where there is demand for both skilled and unskilled workers. Cities that attract large numbers of immigrants are called **gateway cities**.

Immigrants contribute to a gateway city by performing necessary jobs and by paying taxes. They also pay rent, buy homes, and purchase goods, all of which feed the local economy. They often revive city neighborhoods by starting new businesses and renovating buildings. Equally significant are their cultural contributions. Residents of a gateway city might listen to reggae music from Jamaica, eat Vietnamese spring rolls, or watch baseball players from the Dominican Republic.

CHALLENGES AND REWARDS OF MIGRATION

At age 12, Luincys Fernandez (fer-NAN-dez) migrated to the United States from the Dominican Republic. She recalls her struggle to learn English in school: "I became mute. I just listened and listened and I couldn't figure it out, not even a word of what they were saying." Learning a new language is just one challenge immigrants face. You'll find out more about the challenges—and rewards—of migration as you read about two cities with large migrant populations: Mexico City in North America and Amsterdam in Europe.

Explore the Issue

1. **Analyze Causes** What are some push-pull factors that lead people to migrate?

2. **Make Inferences** Why might the United States attract many immigrants?

Centers of Mig

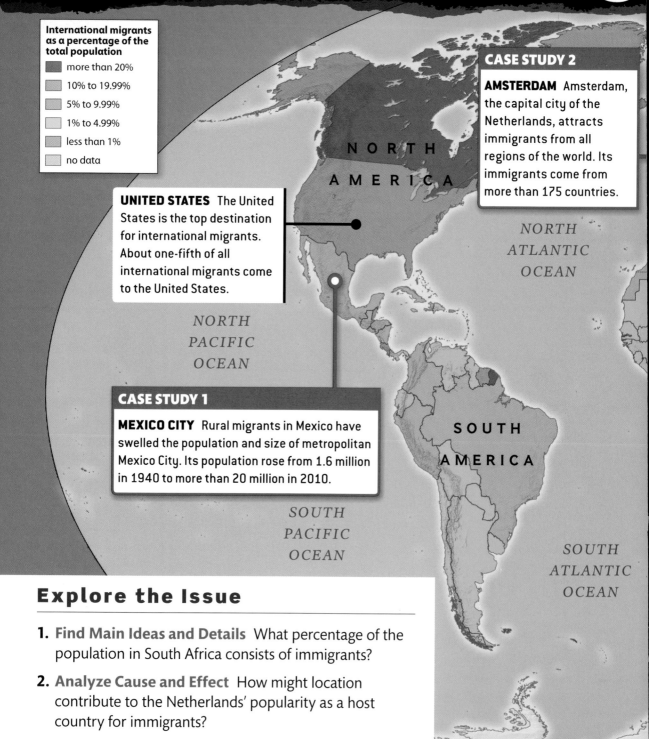

International migrants as a percentage of the total population

- more than 20%
- 10% to 19.99%
- 5% to 9.99%
- 1% to 4.99%
- less than 1%
- no data

CASE STUDY 2

AMSTERDAM Amsterdam, the capital city of the Netherlands, attracts immigrants from all regions of the world. Its immigrants come from more than 175 countries.

UNITED STATES The United States is the top destination for international migrants. About one-fifth of all international migrants come to the United States.

CASE STUDY 1

MEXICO CITY Rural migrants in Mexico have swelled the population and size of metropolitan Mexico City. Its population rose from 1.6 million in 1940 to more than 20 million in 2010.

NORTH AMERICA

NORTH ATLANTIC OCEAN

NORTH PACIFIC OCEAN

SOUTH PACIFIC OCEAN

SOUTH AMERICA

SOUTH ATLANTIC OCEAN

Explore the Issue

1. **Find Main Ideas and Details** What percentage of the population in South Africa consists of immigrants?

2. **Analyze Cause and Effect** How might location contribute to the Netherlands' popularity as a host country for immigrants?

ation

Study the map below to learn about places that have been greatly affected by migration.

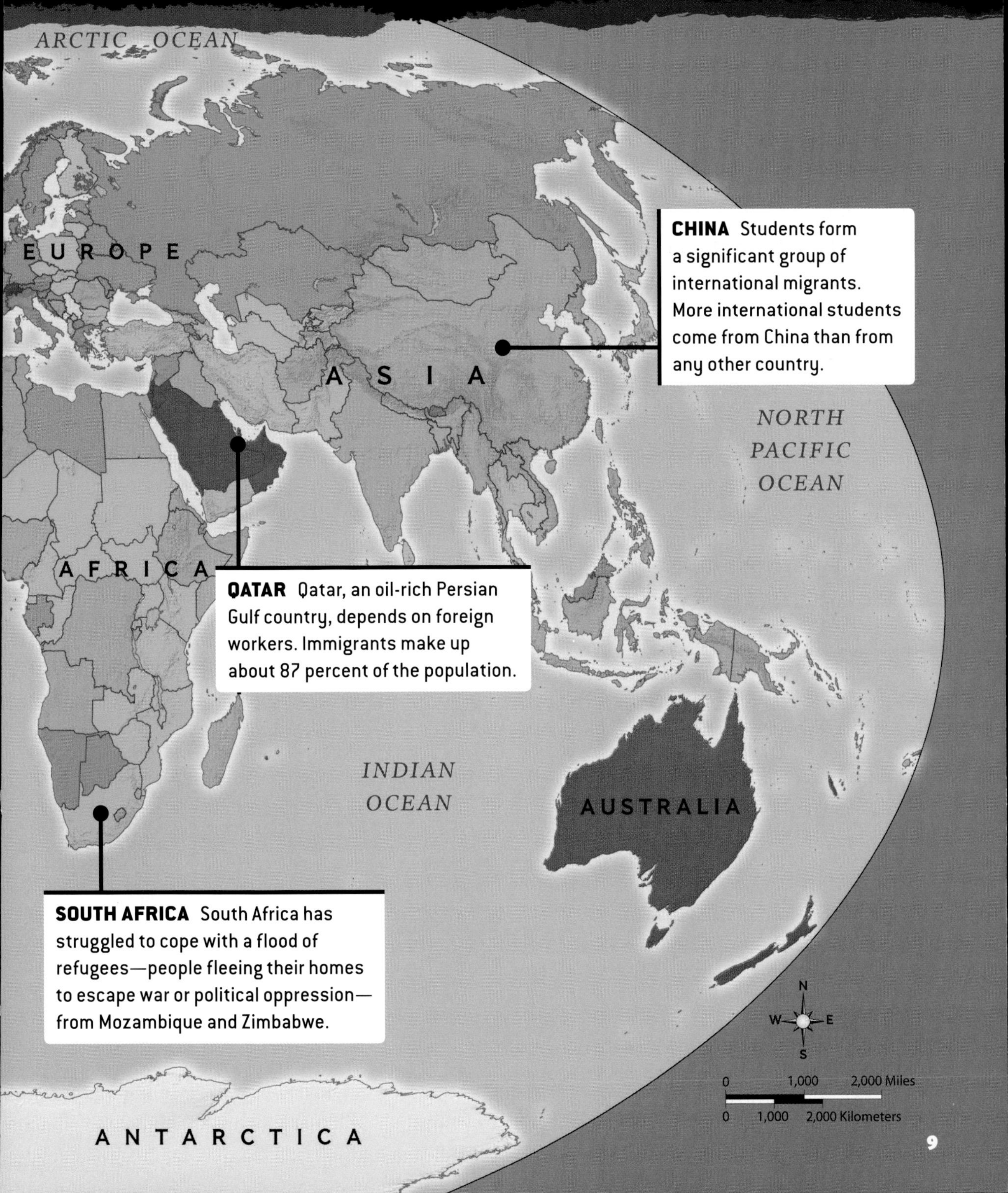

ARCTIC OCEAN

EUROPE

ASIA

AFRICA

NORTH PACIFIC OCEAN

INDIAN OCEAN

AUSTRALIA

ANTARCTICA

CHINA Students form a significant group of international migrants. More international students come from China than from any other country.

QATAR Qatar, an oil-rich Persian Gulf country, depends on foreign workers. Immigrants make up about 87 percent of the population.

SOUTH AFRICA South Africa has struggled to cope with a flood of refugees—people fleeing their homes to escape war or political oppression—from Mozambique and Zimbabwe.

| 0 | 1,000 | 2,000 Miles |
| 0 | 1,000 | 2,000 Kilometers |

N W E S

Sprawling
MEXICO C

Migrants to Mexico City fill a bustling street market where food and a variety of other items can be purchased.

FROM RURAL LIFE TO CITY LIFE

Street vendors in Mexico City sell everything from tamales to car parts. Sounding whistles, bells, and squeeze horns, they're part of the fabric of city life and contribute to Mexico's economy. But some merchants peddle their goods without permits. Having few choices, these merchants are part of Mexico City's **informal economy**. The term means the illegal selling of goods and services without paying taxes.

Part of Mexico City's informal economy, a street vendor earns a living by selling avocados to cope with Mexico's high unemployment rate.

Jobs of all kinds have lured millions of rural Mexicans from the countryside to the city. Mexico City did not have room for this massive **internal migration**—the movement of people within a country's borders. With few resources, the migrants built rows of shacks spreading ever farther on the city's outskirts.

This unchecked development raises one of the issues of migration. It led some observers to label Mexico City an urban disaster in the early 1980s. But in recent years, that opinion has changed. People have worked together to improve the quality of life in the sprawling city.

STRUGGLING TO SURVIVE

A combination of push and pull factors led many waves of rural migrants to pour into Mexico City after 1940. The chief push factors were a lack of available farmland and lack of jobs in rural areas. One migrant who came to Mexico City in 1965 explained simply, "If we'd stayed in the country, my family would have starved."

During the mid-1900s, industrial development in Mexico City created a huge demand for labor. Rural migrants flocked to the city for the jobs. As the economy cycled up and down through the years, the migration continued. When jobs weren't available in the formal economy, people created their own jobs in the informal economy. By the late 2000s, Mexico City's informal economy employed about 40 to 60 percent of the workforce.

EXPANDING MEXICO CITY

As migrants flowed to Mexico City, the population skyrocketed. Between 1940 and 1980, it grew from 1.6 million to about 14 million. Today, the metropolitan population is more than 20 million—about the same as Australia. Mexico City is one of the largest cities in the world. Much of Mexico City's population increase has been due to migration from rural areas.

Just as migrants created their own jobs, many also constructed their own houses using whatever land and supplies were available. Vast shantytowns developed on the city's outskirts where zoning laws did not exist to regulate the construction. Many *barrios* (BAHR-ee-ohs) lacked running water, sewage systems, electricity, and access to mass transit. (*Barrios* are districts of a city in a Spanish-speaking country.) The disorderly urban sprawl overflowed into villages that were once far from the city. **Urban sprawl** is the spread of urban development beyond a city's official boundaries. The lack of planning caused major problems in transportation, sanitation, and water supply.

RISING FROM THE RUBBLE

In the 1980s, Mexico City was almost out of control. Strangely enough, a natural disaster helped change the city. In 1985, a massive earthquake leveled over 100,000 houses and hundreds of public buildings. The quake spurred citizens to action. People organized to deal with the disaster and became more politically active. New building regulations were established, and the federal government gave up ownership of banks and other businesses. The political and economic changes helped transform some communities.

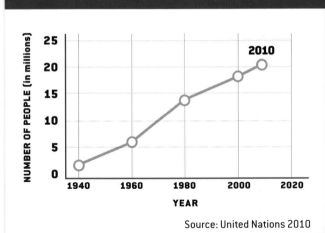

POPULATION GROWTH OF MEXICO CITY, 1940 TO 2010

Source: United Nations 2010

One example of transformation was the suburb of Neza. With 2.7 million people, Neza was labeled the world's largest slum in the mid-1980s. Today, in contrast, the suburb has a thriving economy and numerous colleges.

Migrants from rural areas who have moved to Mexico City use industrial cardboard and boxes to build their homes.

13

Today, over 83 percent
of Mexico's people live
in urban areas.

Internal migration has caused
Mexico City's population to swell to
more than 20 million. It is now one of
the largest cities in the world.

GETTING A GRIP ON URBAN SPRAWL

One problem in solving Mexico City's urban sprawl is the divided government. The city itself falls within the Federal District—the place where the federal government of Mexico is located. However, its suburbs are mostly in the states of Mexico and Hidalgo. The various governmental units often fail to coordinate their policies and programs.

In 2001, the Federal District began a program to replace single-family housing in the inner city with new apartment buildings. At the same time, it limited construction in surrounding neighborhoods. The aim was to increase population density in the central part of the city. **Population density** is the number of people in a specific area. The program also provided loans and expert advice to individuals to improve existing housing in the city. Meanwhile, huge subdivisions with affordable, mass-produced housing sprang up in the suburbs. Even with all the new construction, however, informal developments still account for about half of the new housing built in the metropolitan area.

OPPORTUNITY KNOCKS

Rural migration has also caused the populations of other cities in Mexico to swell. In fact, the migration of people from rural areas to cities and to suburbs has occurred all over the world. The result is crowded cities and empty countrysides. Today, over 83 percent of Mexico's people live in urban areas.

Despite the problems of urban life, many rural migrants to Mexico City have improved their lives over time. As parents struggle to save money, their children are able to gain an education and find higher-paying jobs. "The city offers opportunity," says one rural migrant who makes a living peddling newspapers and gum on the downtown streets of Mexico City.

Explore the Issue

1. **Find Main Ideas and Details** What problems has rural migration caused in the metropolitan area of Mexico City?

2. **Identify Problems and Solutions** How has the city tried to solve its problems?

THE DIVERSE CITY
of
Amsterda

The city of Amsterdam is famous for its wide variety of ethnic groups. More than a quarter of the residents in Amsterdam were born outside the Netherlands.

THE WORLD IN A CITY

Merhaba. Guten Tag. Nei Hou. Bonjour. Hallo. That's "Hello" in Turkish, German, Cantonese, French, and Dutch—just a smattering of the languages you might hear on the streets of Amsterdam. Located in northwestern Europe, Amsterdam is the capital of the Netherlands.

There are more than 190 countries in the world, and Amsterdam's people come from more than 175 of them. More than 28 percent of the city's residents were born in another country. Amsterdam is famous for the **diversity**, or wide variety, of its ethnic groups. In fact, Amsterdam is considered a hyperdiverse (hy-pur-doh-VURS) gateway city. *Hyperdiverse* means its large immigrant population comes from all regions of the world. In a hyperdiverse city, at least 9.5 percent of the total population was born in another country, and immigrants from no single country make up a quarter or more of the immigrant population.

Immigrants play a big part in Amsterdam's economy and cultural life. But many immigrants remain isolated within their own groups. This lack of **integration**—or failure to unify groups of people within a society—worries many native Dutch. They fear the country is becoming fragmented, or divided into many different groups.

TAKING FLIGHT

The largest immigrant groups in Amsterdam come from Suriname (sur-oh-NAH-moh) in northern South America, Morocco in northern Africa, and Turkey in Southwest Asia. These countries have less developed economies and lower living standards than the Netherlands. Many people *emigrate*, or move away, from these countries because there are not enough jobs or the wages are low. They then *immigrate*, or move to a host country, such as the Netherlands.

Many more people want to migrate to Amsterdam than the country can accept. As a result, a portion of the immigrants in Amsterdam are illegal. Illegal immigrants are those who enter or stay in a host country without legal permission. They leave their home countries for the same reasons legal migrants do—to escape poverty, war, or political strife.

Immigrants play an important role in Amsterdam's economy and cultural life.

AMSTERDAM'S APPEAL

Amsterdam has a long history of attracting immigrants. Migrants flock to the city for its freedom, tolerance of other cultures and religions, and high standard of living.

Many of Amsterdam's migrants come from former colonies of the Netherlands. The South American country of Suriname, for example, was a Dutch colony until it became independent in 1975. Many Surinamese then migrated because they feared Suriname might become politically unstable and poorer after independence. Their Dutch citizenship and familiarity with Dutch culture made Amsterdam a comfortable choice of destination for Surinamese immigrants.

In the 1960s and early 1970s, businesses recruited immigrants to fill labor shortages in Amsterdam. The Dutch thought these **guest workers** would one day return to their home countries, but many decided instead to stay and to bring their families to Amsterdam. Family migration, one type of chain migration, accounts for a large portion of the immigration to Amsterdam. In **chain migration**, established migrants help others from their home country settle in a new place.

FACING CHALLENGES

Immigrants around the world face similar challenges. They must find a place to live and a job. They must learn to navigate around a new city. They may need to learn a new language and a new system of money. For many, it's like starting life all over.

In Amsterdam, immigrants tend to cluster together in specific neighborhoods where fellow migrants from their home country can help them get started. Emigrants from Ghana, for example, have established their own community in a neighborhood called Bijlmermeer (beel-mer-MEER), which they call "little Africa." They have set up their own churches and started small businesses that sell African products. Like many other immigrant groups in Amsterdam, the Ghanaians tend to maintain their native customs and stay within their own community.

Amsterdam is the capital of the Netherlands and has been a cultural crossroads for much of its history.

People of many ethnic groups stroll along the market streets in a multicultural area of Amsterdam known as "Indische Buurt."

A waitress serves drinks in an open-air café in Amsterdam. Immigrants have helped Amsterdam's economy grow by starting new businesses.

Multiculturalism has shaped the workplace in the Netherlands, including in this pharmacy where a Muslim woman works.

HELPING IMMIGRANTS SUCCEED

The government, churches, and community organizations in Amsterdam provide many types of aid to immigrants. Despite this help, many immigrants are poor and live in cramped housing. Some have difficulty finding or keeping jobs.

Still, many immigrants succeed over time, and their children become educated, acquiring the skills needed for higher-paying jobs. Immigrants in Amsterdam have been elected to public offices and hold jobs at every skill level.

Immigrants aid Amsterdam's economy by performing necessary jobs and starting new businesses. Many boost their home country's economy as well by sending money to family members there.

THE FUTURE OF IMMIGRATION

Public support for immigration in the Netherlands has declined in recent years. Since the early 2000s, the Netherlands has instituted stronger restrictions on immigration. Its current immigration policy gives preference to highly skilled workers, called "knowledge migrants." However, citizens of countries in the European Union, to which the Netherlands belongs, can move freely among the member countries. This policy makes it harder for the Dutch government to control immigration.

Until the early 2000s, the Dutch government supported a policy referred to as **multiculturalism** (mul-tee-KUL-chur-ohl-iz-ohm), which encouraged the various immigrant groups to maintain their own cultures and languages. Initially, this policy fit with the belief that most guest workers would return to their home countries one day. After many did not return, the government increasingly focused on integration. Whatever the official policies, however, Amsterdam's streets remain multicultural and the city promotes its remarkable diversity.

Explore the Issue

1. **Find Main Ideas and Details** Why is Amsterdam called a hyperdiverse global city?

2. **Compare and Contrast** How does supporting multiculturalism differ from promoting integration in the Netherlands?

Tracing Migration Through DNA

WHERE DO WE COME FROM?

People have always wondered where they come from and how they got to where they are today. Research conducted in the 1980s provided support for a remarkable theory. Many human beings came from a group of African ancestors, some of whom began an incredible migration from Africa about 60,000 years ago. Eventually, their descendants spread out all over the world.

For decades, scientists have tried to piece together the story of human migration from fossils and objects left behind by our ancestors. But there are big gaps in the history. Now, scientists are opening a wider window on the past by analyzing DNA. **DNA** is the material in a cell that contains genetic information. A research project initiated by the National Geographic Society—called the Genographic (jene-oh-GRAF-ik) Project—aims to chart the migratory history of human beings by analyzing the DNA of indigenous populations and the general public. When scientists find the same genetic marker in the DNA of two people, they can conclude that those two people share a common ancestor.

STUDYING GENETIC MAKEUP

Dr. Spencer Wells is a geneticist, author, and documentary filmmaker whose interest in biology and history began in childhood. Today, Wells is a National Geographic Explorer-in-Residence who heads the Genographic Project. He proudly describes the project as "a dream come true."

Wells has been on a fast track since his youth. He enrolled in college at age 16 and graduated three years later. While training at Stanford University's School of Medicine, he decided to focus his career on studying the genetic makeup of indigenous populations. Through field studies in which he gathered DNA for analysis, he began answering questions about early human migration. His studies formed the basis for his award-winning book and film *The Journey of Man: A Genetic Odyssey*.

The Genographic Project expands upon Wells's early field studies. Since the start of the project, Wells has traveled to more than 35 countries, including Chad, Tajikistan, Morocco, and Papua New Guinea.

WHAT DNA REVEALS

"The greatest history book ever written is the one hidden in our DNA," says Wells. Through the Genographic Project, Wells hopes to decode that language and reveal the history.

The Genographic Project began in 2005. It is a multiyear research effort with three parts. In one part, a team of international researchers collaborates with and collects DNA from groups of indigenous peoples around the world. In another part, the general public is invited to buy a Genographic Project Participation Kit and send in a DNA sample for analysis.

Scientists then use computers to analyze historical patterns in the DNA collected from both indigenous peoples and the general public. The scientists look for **genetic markers**, which are genetic changes that are distinctive in different populations of people. These markers can reveal the genetic groups that a person descended from—all the way back to a common African ancestor.

TRACING AN INDIVIDUAL'S MIGRATION

The third part of the Genographic Project involves the money raised from the sale of the Genographic Project kits. The money supports conservation work with traditional peoples and pays for additional project research.

Individuals who want to participate can purchase kits through the Genographic Project's Web site at www.genographic.com. They then send in a painless cheek-swab sample for analysis. The results show the migration paths that their ancient ancestors followed many thousands of years ago. They will even learn what percentages of their genome are associated with different parts of the world. The results do not lead all the way to recent relatives, however. Individuals can learn about the recent migrations of their ancestors by interviewing parents and grandparents. Many people discover incredible migration stories of their own.

Explore the Issue

1. **Summarize** To which continent can all human beings trace their ancestry?

2. **Pose Questions** What questions do you have about the Genographic Project?

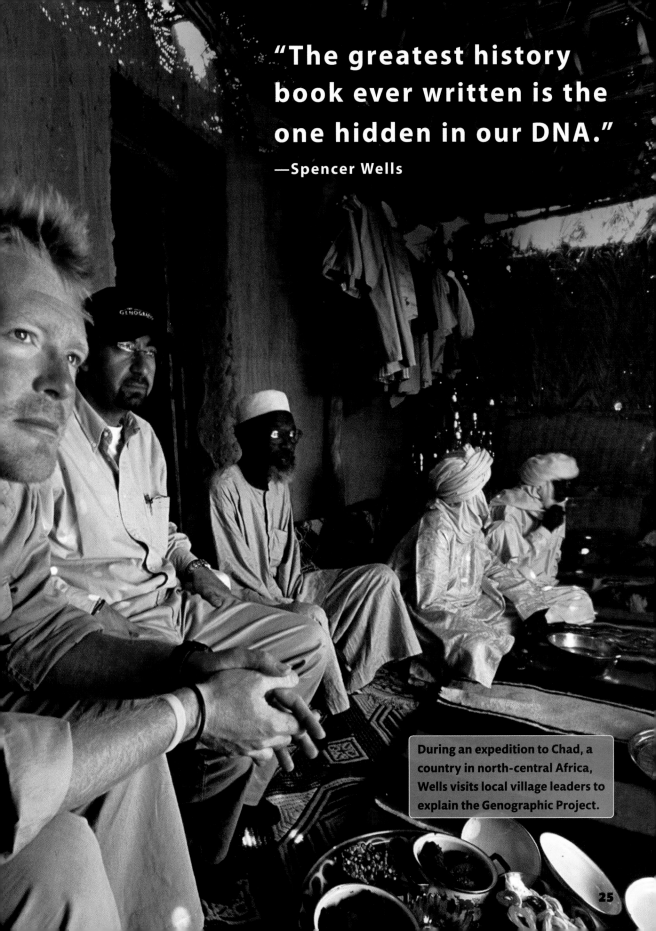

"The greatest history book ever written is the one hidden in our DNA."

—Spencer Wells

During an expedition to Chad, a country in north-central Africa, Wells visits local village leaders to explain the Genographic Project.

What Can I DO?

Stage a Culture Fair

How much do you know about the native cultures of immigrants to the United States? Find out more about the culture of one group, and use what you have learned to prepare a presentation. Then work with your classmates to stage a culture fair in your school to celebrate cultural diversity.

DISCUSS

- Conduct a class discussion and create a list of immigrant groups to feature in a culture fair. Your list should include as many different groups as possible.

- Form pairs and choose one immigrant group to research.

- Decide what kind of presentation you want to create, such as a poster or a multimedia slide show.

RESEARCH

- Use the Internet and library to research your immigrant group. Look at the census data for your city or state to see what immigrant populations live in your area.

- Find out about the language, customs, music, foods, and other features of the group's culture.

- Learn about the group's migration paths around the world.

Wearing costumes, Irish step dancers perform during a St. Patrick's Day parade in Denver, Colorado. Dancers must hold their arms straight down while they perform complicated steps.

CREATE

- Brainstorm titles for your presentation and sketch a layout.

- Write the text and find or create visuals for your presentation.

- Determine what other items to include with your presentation. For example, you might include a map, samples of food, a recording of music, or a dance demonstration. You might wish to include written or spoken language of the culture represented.

SHARE

- Work with your teacher to schedule a time for a schoolwide culture fair to share presentations.

- Take photos or digitally record the presentation as a record of your work.

- Conduct a class discussion on this question: What aspects of other cultures do you find most interesting? Why?

Research & WRITE
Narrative

Write a Narrative

What's it like to migrate to a foreign country where you don't speak the language? What happens on the first day of school or when you go to a store? Interview a classmate, relative, or acquaintance who is an immigrant. Use what you learn in the interview to write a narrative about the migration experience.

RESEARCH

Identify someone who relocated to your community from another country, and request permission to write about his or her experience.

- Make a list of questions, and schedule a time to interview the person.
- Record your conversation or take notes.

If you're an immigrant, you might write about your own experience.

DRAFT

Use your recording or notes to plan the narrative.

- As you draft the first paragraph, establish the context and point of view and introduce the narrator.
- In the body paragraph, create dialogue and use description to develop the experiences or events.
- As you write, use transition words and phrases, such as *before*, *finally*, and *the next time*, to help sequence events and signal a shift in time or setting.
- Write a conclusion that follows from and reflects on the experiences or events.

REVISE & EDIT

Review your draft to make sure your writing is clear.

- Did you set the context and introduce the narrator?
- Do the events in your narrative follow a logical sequence?
- Does the dialogue help develop the experience? Do the details describe the experience clearly?
- Did you use a variety of transition words and phrases to convey the sequence of events and to signal shifts in time and setting?
- Have you included enough descriptive details and sensory language to capture the migration experience?

Revise the draft to improve the narrative flow. Then check the story for correct spelling, capitalization, and punctuation. Are ethnic names and places spelled correctly? Is the dialogue realistic? Do you conclude with your thoughts about the immigrant experience?

PUBLISH & PRESENT

Add a photograph or illustration to your narrative. Then create a booklet of migration narratives by combining your story with those of your classmates. As a class, decide on a title for the booklet, and ask a volunteer to design a cover. Share the printed booklet by reading the stories in class, or take turns bringing the booklet home for family members to read.

Visual GLOSSARY

informal economy

DNA

chain migration *n.*, a way established migrants help others from their home country settle in a new place

diversity *n.*, a wide variety

DNA *n.*, the material in a cell that contains genetic information

gateway city *n.*, a city that attracts a large number of immigrants

genetic marker *n.*, a genetic change that is distinctive in different populations of people

guest worker *n.*, a foreigner who works temporarily in a host country

immigrant *n.*, a person who moves specifically to a new country

informal economy *n.*, the illegal sale of goods and services without paying taxes

integration *n.*, a unity of the groups of people within a society

internal migration *n.*, the movement of people within a country's borders

migrant *n.*, a person who moves from one region or country to another

migration *n.*, the movement of people from one region or country to another

multiculturalism *n.*, a policy of encouraging immigrant groups to maintain their own cultures

population density *n.*, the number of people in a specific area

urban sprawl *n.*, the spread of development beyond a city's official boundaries

gateway city

population density

immigrant

31

INDEX

SKILLS